Castles

Publisher and Creative Director: Nick Wells
Editor: Polly Willis
Picture Research: Gemma Walters
Designer: Vanessa Green
Thanks to: Chris Herbert and Sara Robson

Guy de la Bédoyère (author) lives in Lincolnshire and is a freelance historian, archaeologist, writer and broadcaster with
degrees in history and archaeology from the universities of London and Durham. He has written more than twenty books on
historical subjects as diverse as Roman Britain, the polio vaccine, the Home Front and the Correspondence of Samuel Pepys,
and has contributed to Flame Tree's World History, World Facts and Irish History. His numerous appearances on television
include many spots on Channel 4's archaeology series Time Team. He has also presented live archaeology programmes for
Channel 5, and co-presented a genealogy series for UKTV History.

Picture Credits:
Courtesy of Andy Williams: 12, 13, 16–33, 35–37, 39, 41, 46, 48, 49, 55, 56, 60, 61, 63, 66, 67, 69–73, 77, 78, 80, 81, 83, 86, 89, 90,
91, 93, 96, 102–111, 113–117, 122. Courtesy of Corbis: 34, 112, 120, 121, 125, 137, 142, 143, 147, 150, 153, 156, 159–162, 164, 167,
170, 173, 175, 181, 188, 192. Courtesy of Istockphoto: 14, 38, 40, 42, 47, 53, 59, 62, 64, 84, 85, 88, 94, 95, 99, 124, 130, 131, 134, 176,
179. Courtesy of Topham Picturepoint: 15, 50, 58, 65, 68, 76, 82, 98, 123, 126–128, 135, 136, 139, 140, 141, 144, 149, 151, 152, 157,
158, 165, 166, 168, 171, 177, 185–187, 189, 193, 194, 196, 197

ISBN-13: 978-0-7607-8911-7
ISBN-10: 0-7607-8911-8

A copy of the CIP data for this book is available from the British Library.

Printed and bound in China

1   3   5   7   9   10   8   6   4   2

CASTLES

by Guy de la Bédoyère

BARNES & NOBLE
NEW YORK

Contents

CONTENTS

Introduction

Our word 'castle' comes from the Latin *castellum*, meaning a 'castle' or 'fortress'. What we mean by a castle is a large fortified building or group of buildings, usually belonging to the European Middle Ages of the eleventh to fifteenth centuries, and typically with massive walls reinforced with towers and gates. Towering above the landscape they are the greatest and most visible remnants of Europe's volatile history and feudal societies, forming an evocative testimony of the people who built them and lived in them. So it is no surprise that many of the castles in this book such as Windsor Castle in England, Muiderslot in Holland and Bran Castle in Romania are amongst the most popular monuments in their respective countries and visited by thousands of people every year.

The types of castles and details of their design change a great deal, depending on where they were built and when they were built. Castles were designed to defend important places, so they had to protect their garrisons and their equipment. They also acted as homes for their owners. That meant being able to resist attackers who might lay sieges for months or even years, and who might try and break their way in using artillery and by digging under the castle walls. Their vast walls had slit windows so that defenders could fire arrows at attackers. The tops of the walls had crenellations to protect defenders and overhangs so that boiling oil and other weapons could be thrown at anyone attacking.

Castles developed because in the Middle Ages Europe was broken up into kingdoms and other small states, which were themselves all broken up into territory ruled by local barons who had their own private armies. In a feudal society castles were how these kings and barons showed their status, charged taxes, controlled the local population, protected their interests and guarded their land. All castle builders wanted one thing above all: impregnability. An impregnable castle meant its owner could do more or less what he pleased. Castle design steadily evolved in an effort to find the most effective and durable way of resisting enemy attack.

Half the secret was choosing the right spot. Castles were often built overlooking a river crossing, a road, mountain pass or beside a harbour. The castle and its garrison could prevent an enemy passing or seizing control of a port, and cut off his supplies. It was essential to find a spot that also provided solid rock foundations, a supply of fresh water and a source of building materials close by. A series of castles like this built in key strategic locations could control a whole country.

In the tenth and eleventh centuries castles were relatively simple. The main castle building, the keep (originally known as a donjon), was built on top of an earthen mound called a motte. Keeps could be circular or square. One of the most important surviving examples of an eleventh-century square keep is the White Tower in the Tower of London. Both were built by the Normans soon after William I's conquest of England in 1066.

The simplest keeps had one room per storey, which accommodated the lord and a few other people, so these were soon added to with a courtyard protected by a curtain wall (or bailey). Here the garrison could find protection, and so could animals needed for food and transport. Sometimes Roman forts were adapted for this purpose. The medieval castles at Pevensey and Portchester used the walls of Roman forts at both places as their baileys.

The most sophisticated castles, and Dover is one of them, had an inner and an outer bailey, providing a whole series of zones which an attacker would have to fight his way through. Castles that were not built on hills or above rivers could be reinforced with a deep ditch called a moat (sometimes flooded). A moat helped protect the castle even better, by limiting the number of ways in and preventing attackers from tunnelling under the walls.

By the late twelfth century castles were beginning to become more complicated. The Crusades in the Holy Land had led to a vast improvement in castle design, where being able to withstand sieges for years was vital. Building projecting towers into massive outer walls was found to be an excellent way to do this.

Krak des Chevaliers in Syria was supposed to be able to accommodate 3,000 soldiers for five years. Crusaders brought home these ideas. Framlingham in Suffolk is an early example of this new style with large projecting towers built in the curtain wall, though in this case they were square.

In the thirteenth century castle building became even more sophisticated. Square towers and keeps were more easily damaged if a single corner was undermined. So new shapes were tried such as the Emperor Frederick II's Castel del Monte in Italy with its remarkable octagonal keep. Some of the greatest castles of the age were built by Edward I in Wales and these show how round towers in curtain walls had become one of the most defining characteristics. Conwy Castle in Wales has eight massive towers in its

huge walls containing the inner and outer wards, as well as two flanking outworks called barbicans with their own curtain walls and round towers. Barbicans provided another line of defence around a weak feature like a gateway. Beaumaris Castle in Wales, built about 1295–1300, is a classic example of the new design because it is symmetrical, and also has a massively elaborated gatehouse, which was always the weakest part of a castle's defences. Poland's Malbork is a complex of three castles and defences built by an order of holy knights.

Inside these great castles were all the facilities needed by a king or a lord to feed, house and protect his household and retainers. There was a great hall for eating and meeting, a kitchen, quarters for the nobles, barracks for the soldiers, storerooms for food and equipment, stables and a chapel. The king or lord was unlikely to be in the castle at all times. For the rest of the year a smaller garrison kept the castle running and ready for his arrival.

The fourteenth century saw a massive change in the purpose of castles. Perhaps the most extreme example is the papal palace at Avignon, built for defence but also for pure luxury. Bodiam Castle in Sussex is one of the best-preserved castles in Europe. Built in 1385 to act as an impregnable fortress but also as a home, it was one of the last conventional castles built to act in both roles. There was also a portent for the future. Bodiam had gunports because gunpowder had arrived in Europe. But the guns available at the time were far too small to represent a serious threat to castles. The decline in castle building had more to do with changes in society and warfare. Castles were extremely expensive to build and maintain. Only kings could afford to build them in large numbers but even they struggled sometimes. Beaumaris, for example, was never finished because Edward I had gone to fight a war in Scotland and had taken his resources with him. Sieges were giving way to fighting things out on battlefields and private armies were being outlawed.

By the fifteenth century traditional castles were becoming out of date. Feudalism was in decline as local barons lost their power to the crown. Castles gave way to fortified houses, which were built to look like castles but had none of the massive fortifications of places such as Beaumaris or Caernarfon. Frederick II and Christian IV's castle at Kronborg was still defended, but it had all the appearance and pretensions of a Renaissance palace despite having an important role guarding the narrow waterway between Denmark and

Sweden. Other castles still had vast walls and projecting towers, but the walls were much thinner and even the towers were filled with living quarters. Before long manor houses were being built that made no pretence to being castles like France's Château de Chaumont.

By the sixteenth century castles were mainly a thing of the past, though Henry VIII built a new series of coastal forts like Deal that inherited some of the old tradition. By the nineteenth century castles had become the stuff of romantic legend, leading to the astonishing new fantasy castles built in Europe such as Ludwig II of Bavaria's celebrated Neuschwanstein, or Carol I of Romania's Peles. But the great medieval castles still had last acts to play. In the English Civil War of the 1640s castles were used as strongholds especially by the Royalists, often falling to the more powerful guns of the era, while in Europe others served in the Thirty Years War of 1618–48, the Napoleonic Wars and some even in the Second World War. Pevensey Castle was refortified in case of a German invasion in 1940. That of course is why so many of the castles featured in this book survive – they were built to last.

England

England's extraordinary castles dominate the skyline in the towns, villages and natural features they were built on. Many date back to the days of the Norman Conquest in 1066 and the distribution of lands by William the Conqueror amongst his friends and supporters, who promptly secured their new possessions with castles.

The most famous of all is William's own Tower of London with its unique story at the heart of British history, but they also include castles like Chepstow, where the keep survives today almost in its original form. Together they all tell the story of how castles played a dramatic role in the tussle between the kings and their barons, and what happened as England became a more settled place and castles became fortified manor houses.

It was Henry VIII, facing the furious Catholic France and Spain after his reformation, who built a new type of coastal artillery fort to protect against invasion. In a curious twist of fate the only time many English castles saw action was during the Civil War of the 1640s when the Royalists held them against besieging Parliamentary armies. After then, many castles fell into ruin becoming picturesque relics of medieval times or were rebuilt to find a new lease of life as stately homes.

DUNSTANBURGH CASTLE

Northumberland

Dunstanburgh Castle lies by the sea at the top of a steep cliff protecting it on two sides. Originally built between 1315 and 1325 by Thomas, Earl of Lancaster (1277–1322) a nephew of Edward I (1272–1307) the castle with its magnificent gatehouse with two D-shaped towers protected Thomas from the king and Scottish raiders. John of Gaunt (1349–99) redesigned Dunstanburgh with an outer and inner bailey. Today the fourteenth-century Lilburn Tower is one of the best-preserved parts of the castle.

ALNWICK CASTLE

Northumberland

Yves de Vescy, Baron of Alnwick, started the castle in 1096. In 1309 Alnwick passed into the Percy family, one of the most powerful in England, and later the earls of Northumberland. The Percys remodelled the castle but after the Middle Ages it fell into ruins, though parts remain, including the Abbot's Tower. In 1750 Sir Hugh Smithson, future Duke of Northumberland, restored it and so did his descendant, the fourth Duke. Today the Alnwick is the second biggest inhabited castle in Britain.

BAMBURGH CASTLE
Northumberland

Bamburgh lies by the sea on a basalt outcrop. The original keep was built by Henry II (1154–89). During the Wars of the Roses in 1464 the Lancastrian Henry VI took refuge here from his enemy, the Yorkist Edward IV. Henry was defeated when Edward badly damaged the castle with cannon fire, making it the first English castle to fall to gunpowder. Bamburgh remained in ruins until the 1890s when William, first Baron Armstrong, an armaments manufacturer, bought and restored the castle.

CHILLINGHAM CASTLE
Northumberland

Chillingham, built in the 1100s, was converted into a castle in 1344 by Sir Thomas Grey who erected four corner towers, crenellations, an inner courtyard and an outer curtain wall. In 1536 the castle was damaged by cannon fire during the Pilgrimage of Grace when Catholic rebels protested against the Reformation. Edward I stayed here in 1298 and James I in 1617. The castle was restored in the eighteenth and nineteenth centuries. Chillingham is still lived in by descendants of the Grey family.

BARNARD CASTLE
Durham

Built by about 1125 on a steep bank of the River Tees, Barnard Castle belonged to Bernard de Bailleul and his descendants, the powerful Baliol family who included the kings of Scotland. Later it was owned by the Neville family and passed to Richard III (1483–85) who married Anne Neville. After he was killed at the Battle of Bosworth the castle fell into ruins. In 1630 Sir Henry Vane bought the site and used it as a quarry to build nearby Raby Castle.

DURHAM CASTLE
Durham

Today part of the University of Durham, Durham Castle has remained in continuous use since Norman times. Built to defend the city from Scottish raids, the castle guarded the entrance to the narrow peninsula in a loop of the River Wear. Parts of the Norman gate survive. Much of the castle was restored in the seventeenth century. The prominent octagonal keep was built by Bishop Hatfield (1345–81). It became the bishop's palace but the keep fell into ruin, being restored in 1840.

BROUGHAM CASTLE

Cumbria

Sitting on the corner of a Roman fort by the River Eamont, Brougham Castle was built in 1214 by Robert de Vieuxpoint. In about 1300 Robert de Clifford (1273–1314), who was constantly fighting off Scottish raids, improved the castle's defences and replaced the timber curtain wall with a stone one. Brougham played an important part in the Wars of the Roses. In 1643 Lady Anne Clifford inherited Brougham and restored it, but after her death in 1676 it fell into ruin.

RICHMOND CASTLE
North Yorkshire

William I gave the land here overlooking the River Swale and the town of Richmond to Alan the Red of Brittany. Alan began the castle in 1071, making it one of the oldest in England. In the 1100s the keep, the best-preserved part, was built over the original gatehouse. Two Scottish kings, William the Lion of Scotland, and David II, were imprisoned here (in 1174 and 1346 respectively). Charles I stayed here in 1647 after surrendering to the Scots during the Civil War.

BOLTON CASTLE
North Yorkshire

Bolton Castle towers over the village of Castle Bolton. In 1379 Richard II's chancellor Richard, Baron Scrope, started converting his manor house into a castle. Each of the four entrances into the wings from the courtyard had its own portcullis. Elizabeth I imprisoned Mary Queen of Scots here in 1568. As a Royalist Scrope was besieged in the English Civil War until starved into surrendering in 1645 by the Parliamentarians. A tower collapsed in 1762 but otherwise the castle has survived remarkably well.

HELMSLEY CASTLE
North Yorkshire

Helmsley is dominated by its two huge defensive ditches cut into the rock. Walter L'Espec dug them to protect his new timber castle in the early 1100s. The de Roos family inherited the castle in 1154 and rebuilt it in stone adding the towers and other buildings. Helmsley later passed to the Manners family who converted it into a Tudor country house in the 1560s. Helmsley only saw action in 1644, falling to Parliament after a six-month siege.

LUDLOW CASTLE
Shropshire

Called by Daniel Defoe 'the very perfection of decay', Ludlow was founded by the de Lacy family in the late eleventh century to guard the Welsh Marches. Constantly at the centre of events in this dangerous region, Ludlow was sacked in 1459 during the Wars of the Roses, passing to the crown in 1461, and besieged in the Civil War. Until 1689 Wales was governed from Ludlow, but afterwards the castle fell into ruin as locals stripped it for building materials. The Princes killed in the Tower of London in 1485 grew up here, and Henry VII's eldest son Arthur died here in 1502.

ACTON BURNELL CASTLE
Shropshire

Built in attractive red sandstone, Acton Burnell was a fortified manor house built in 1284 by Robert Burnell, Chancellor of England, Bishop of Bath and Wells, and wealthy landowner (he had 82 manors in 19 counties). Acton Burnell fell into ruin when a new hall was built in 1814. Only the shell of the manor house with its four corner towers and window openings still stands. Archways were added in the 1800s to turn the ruins into a picturesque garden folly.

BOLSOVER CASTLE
Derbyshire

Bolsover began its life as a conventional Norman motte-and-bailey, built by William Peveril. In 1612 Sir Charles Cavendish bought the castle and began converting it into a fantasy castle in celebration of the age of chivalry. Calling it the 'Little Castle' he decorated it with elaborate fireplaces, ceilings, paintings and gardens. In 1634 Charles I and his court attended a theatrical performance at Bolsover. Modern restoration has revived its Jacobean heyday and today Bolsover is home to concerts, plays and re-enactments.

ELVASTON CASTLE
Derbyshire

The present Elvaston Castle is an eighteenth- and nineteenth-century stately home built by the earls of Harrington, though it stands on a site that dates back to an eleventh-century castle. The fourth Earl had the house converted between 1830 and 1850 into a secluded Gothic paradise for him and his wife, and gardens landscaped. Elvaston fell into decay after the Second World War and although attempts have been made to restore it, the place has defied attempts to find the money.

NEWARK CASTLE

Nottinghamshire

Newark Castle's finest hour was during the English Civil War when it stood firm through three Parliamentary sieges in 1643, 1644 and 1646. Only when Charles I was captured nearby and ordered Newark to surrender did the castle fall. Built originally in 1133 by the Bishop of Lincoln to hold the road to the north, it was owned by the church until Henry VIII seized it in 1547. It was largely demolished after the Civil War but remains an imposing town centre ruin.

BELVOIR CASTLE
Leicestershire

Commanding magnificent views across the local countryside, Belvoir (pronounced 'Beaver') Castle is an equally magnificent building. Unusually it is the fourth castle on the site, even though it has remained the home of the Dukes of Rutland for a thousand years. The first castle was destroyed in the Wars of the Roses, the next in the Civil War and the third by fire in 1816. The present castle, built soon afterwards, preserves fabulous nineteenth-century gardens, interiors and fittings including silks and tapestries.

WARWICK CASTLE
Warwickshire

William the Conqueror built Warwick in timber and earth in 1086. In 1088 it passed to the first Earl of Warwick and over the next three centuries it was substantially rebuilt, climaxing in Thomas de Beauchamp's late-fourteenth-century work which added the two huge towers including the 39-m (128-ft) high Guy's Tower, gatehouse and barbican visible today. In 1750 Capability Brown landscaped the gardens. In 1978 the castle was sold to the Tussaud's group and is today a major historical attraction.

KENILWORTH CASTLE

Warwickshire

EASTNOR CASTLE

Herefordshire

Kenilworth started life as a timber keep in 1116. Seized by Henry II (1154–89) it was completely remodelled in the thirteenth century with epic fortifications. Rebels held out here against Henry III's siege of 1266 for nine months, and only surrendered when disease broke out. A later owner, Elizabeth I's favourite Robert Dudley, Earl of Leicester, added Tudor gardens and architectural features to create a palace fit to entertain her there in 1566, 1568 and 1575 with ruinously expensive pageants.

The nineteenth century was a time when many people fell in love with the romantic ideals of medieval chivalry. Some castles were restored to reflect that but Eastnor was built by the wealthy Earl Somers in 1810 as a brand-new mock castle in medieval style. Designed by the architect Robert Smirke, Eastnor cost the equivalent of £8.5 million and took 250 men six years to build with 4,000 tons of stone. Eastnor boasts a Gothic drawing room designed by Augustus Pugin.

CASTLE RISING
Norfolk

Begun in 1140 by William d'Albini, Castle Rising was always unusually elaborate, being built of imported stone and ornately decorated. In 1331 Edward III gave it to his mother, Queen Isabella, known as the 'She Wolf'. She lived in some luxury here until her death in 1358 when her grandson Edward, the 'Black Prince', took it over. After his death in 1376 the castle fell into ruin. Today the keep magnificently survives to its full original height behind the huge surrounding earthworks.

FRAMLINGHAM CASTLE
Suffolk

A striking example of new castle design with its 12 huge projecting hollow towers in the curtain wall, Framlingham was built between 1189 and 1200 by Roger Bigod, Earl of Norfolk. With no keep, the idea was that all the defensive capability lay in the earthworks and wall. Mary Tudor lived here before becoming queen in 1553. By the late 1500s Framlingham was a prison and in 1664 the great hall was demolished to build a poorhouse. The later 1729 poorhouse survives.

ORFORD CASTLE
Suffolk

KIMBOLTON CASTLE
Cambridgeshire

Henry II built Orford Castle's unusual polygonal and innovative keep between 1165 and 1167 so that he could keep an eye on the troublesome barons of East Anglia. Remarkably, the original construction records have survived. The keep has 21 sides, three projecting towers, a circular interior and rooms on five floors. At 27 m (86 ft) in height the keep commanded exceptional views across Orford Ness and the countryside. All the outbuildings, walls and gates are gone but the keep is almost intact.

Kimbolton is unrecognisable today as the twelfth-century medieval castle and Tudor manor it once was, where Henry VIII's estranged first queen, Catherine of Aragon, was sent in 1534 and where she died in 1536. Parts of the Tudor house survive but Kimbolton was remodelled by Sir John Vanbrugh as a stately home for the Dukes of Manchester, who bought the castle in 1615, between 1690 and 1720. Vanbrugh incorporated crenellations to echo the long-vanished castle. The house is now Kimbolton School.

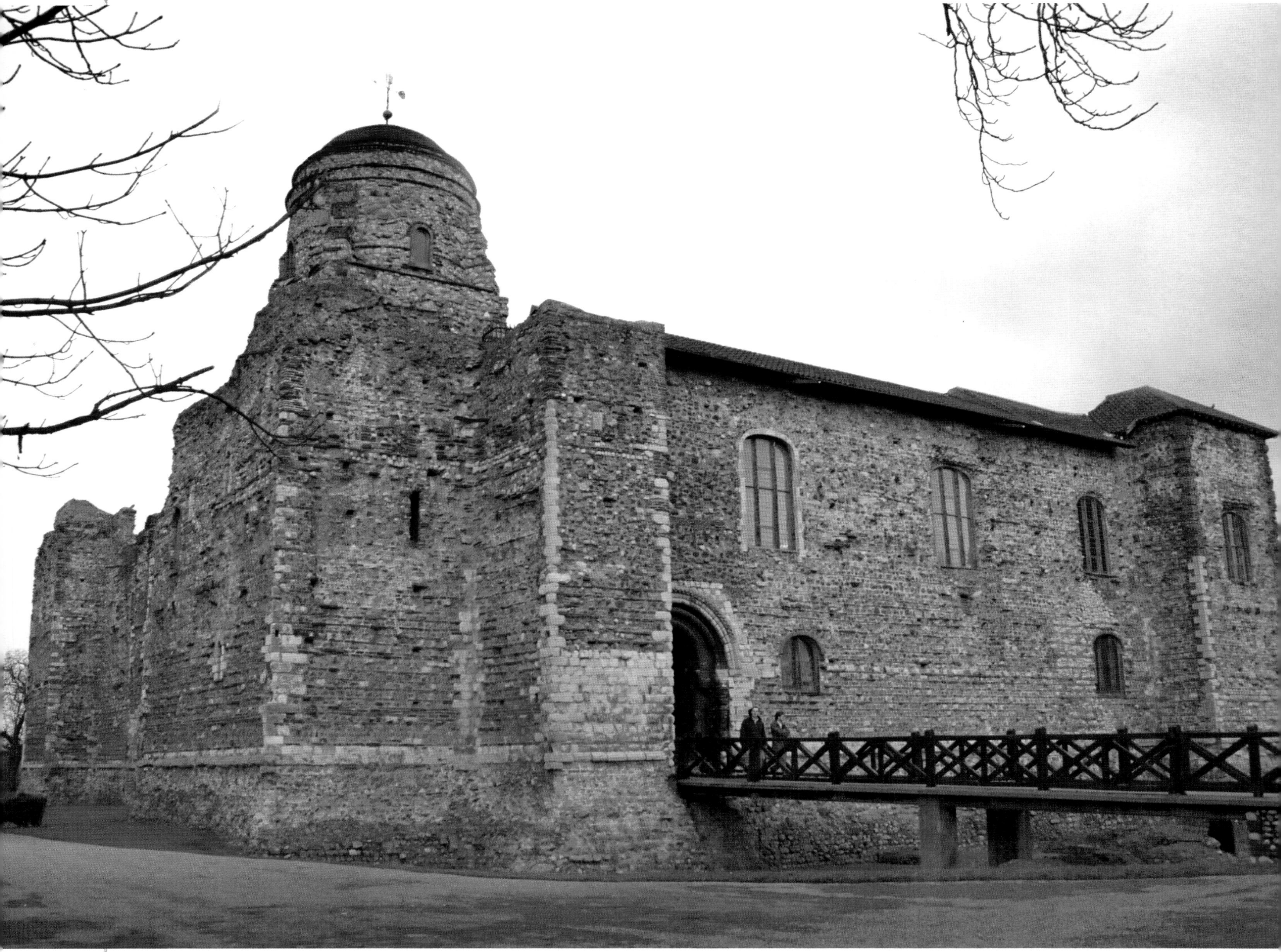

COLCHESTER CASTLE
Essex

Colchester's castle, the largest keep in Britain, has a truly unique history. Its foundations are the vaults of the Roman Temple of Claudius in what was one of Roman Britain's most important cities. The castle was built between 1075 and 1080 by Hugo Dapifer, who used rubble and tile from Roman buildings. In 1645 suspected witches were imprisoned here. In 1683 the castle was reduced in height, and today houses Colchester's museum where artefacts from Britain's oldest city are on display.

HEDINGHAM CASTLE
Essex

Hedingham's 1140 keep, built by Aubrey de Vere and probably designed by the Archbishop of Canterbury, is one of the best-preserved in England. Its second-floor banqueting hall has the largest Norman arch in England. In 1216 King John besieged Hedingham and later Henry VII and Elizabeth I were entertained here. The castle remained in the de Vere family until 1703. Today a descendant owns it. None of the other buildings survive and the keep stands alone in the gardens of a 1719 country house.

TOWER OF LONDON
London

The White Tower keep was begun by William the Conqueror and finished in 1100, but today is surrounded by numerous fortifications and other buildings belonging to its notorious history as a place of imprisonment, torture and execution including that of Queen Anne Boleyn and Lady Jane Grey. The Tower of London was also used as the royal mint, and is today famous for its yeoman warders (the Beefeaters), its ravens and the Crown Jewels, which were famously stolen in 1671 during Charles II's reign.

DONNINGTON CASTLE
Berkshire

Richard Abberbury, justice of Berkshire, Oxfordshire and Wiltshire, was given a licence to turn Donnington into a castle by Richard II in 1386. By Tudor times Donnington was owned by the crown but passed into private hands again before being held by Charles I during the Civil War. The fourteenth-century defences withstood an 18-month siege by the Parliamentarians, and then the Second Battle of Newbury. Donnington was completely demolished in 1646. Nothing now remains of the castle apart from its monumental gatehouse.

WINDSOR CASTLE
Berkshire

The biggest and oldest occupied castle in the world, Windsor was begun by William the Conqueror to guard the western approach to London. Since this time Windsor has constantly been modified, restored and enlarged – mainly by Edward III in the 1360s and Charles II in the 1660s. But even today Windsor still sits within outer walls that run on the original Norman line. In 1992 a catastrophic fire wrecked one-fifth of the Castle, but within five years it had been restored.

WALMER CASTLE
Kent

Henry VIII built Walmer, Deal and Sandown between 1539 and 1540 to defend Kent from possible attack by Spain and France. Designed as a fortified artillery platform, Walmer had a central circular keep and four radiating circular bastions. The Royalist garrison was besieged in 1648 during the Civil War. In 1708 Walmer was made the Lord Warden of the Cinque Ports' residence and became an attractive country home with gardens, used by the Duke of Wellington and the Queen Mother, amongst others.

LEEDS CASTLE

A Saxon wooden castle, built here in AD 857 by a man called Leed, is responsible for this beautiful castle's name. In 1119 a stone castle was built on the island in the lake, added to by Edward I in 1278. Six queens lived here, and in 1520 Henry VIII converted it into a palace for Catherine of Aragon. In the late 1600s Leeds was used to house Dutch and French prisoners-of-war. During the Second World War Leeds served as a weapons research centre. Leeds appears as the ancestral home of the D'Ascoyne family in the famous 1949 Ealing comedy *Kind Hearts and Coronets*.

DOVER CASTLE
Kent

Towering over the busy port of Dover, the site of the castle was vitally important from Roman times to the Second World War. A Roman lighthouse still stands here. William the Conqueror enlarged the Anglo-Saxon castle but it was Henry II whose rebuild in the 1180s created the huge keep and its concentric rings of outer defences that stand today. Underground tunnels from the Napoleonic Wars were used in 1940 as the command centre for evacuating troops from Dunkirk.

HEVER CASTLE
Kent

This elegant and pretty fortified manor house was built in 1270 but by the late 1400s it belonged to the ambitious Boleyn family. Henry VIII's mistresses Mary Boleyn and her sister Anne, later queen and mother of Elizabeth I, grew up here. After Anne's execution in 1536 Henry VIII seized the castle and gave it to his estranged fourth wife Anne of Cleves. In 1903 an American millionaire called William Waldorf bought Hever and restored it, even creating a Tudor-style village for visitors.

CHIDDINGSTONE CASTLE
Kent

DEAL CASTLE
Kent

Originally a medieval manor house, Chiddingstone Castle was rebuilt as a mock-castle in the early eighteenth century, with towers, arched windows and a gatehouse structure. Unfortunately, only part of the house was completed due to spiralling costs. The estate was sold in the 1930s and suffered from neglect until it was bought by Denys Eyre Bower in 1955. A passionate art collector, Eyre Bower opened Chiddingstone to the public so that visitors could view his works of art in the comfortable surroundings of a 'private' home.

Deal was one of several fortified artillery emplacements built round the Kent coast between 1539 and 1540 by Henry VIII to defend England from attack by Catholic France and Spain. Deal is squat and compact, designed to withstand a barrage of cannon fire while its radial bastions served as platforms for 66 pieces of artillery to fire at attackers. Never seeing action in Tudor times, Deal was besieged for three months in the Civil War, and later served in the Napoleonic Wars.

ALLINGTON CASTLE
Kent

Allington started life as a timber castle on a motte, but was converted into a stone castle in 1281 by Stephen of Penchester who was given royal permission to add crenellations and towers. In 1492 it was made into a fortified manor house. A massive fire wrecked Allington in 1600 and only a farmhouse stood amongst the ruins until the explorer and art critic William Martin, Baron Conway of Allington (1856–1937), restored it. In 1951 the Carmelite nuns bought Allington.

ROCHESTER CASTLE
Kent

Rochester commands the vital river crossing over the Medway on the road to London. Its ruinous keep, designed in 1087 by the Archbishop of Canterbury, still stands to full height right next to the cathedral. In 1215 barons who objected to the Magna Carta held out here. King John laid siege and brought a corner tower down by digging a hole underneath and setting fire to the fat from 40 pigs inside. A new circular tower was built in its place.

GUILDFORD CASTLE
Surrey

BODIAM CASTLE
East Sussex

Now in a public garden near Guildford's busy high street, this stone castle replaced a timber keep in the twelfth century. Guildford was a royal castle until Henry III's death in 1272, used for administering Surrey. Later kings preferred a nearby hunting lodge, leaving Guildford falling into decay as a prison. Despite an abortive attempt in 1611 to convert the remains into a house the castle has remained a ruin ever since, leaving it an important example of an original Norman castle.

If ever there was a textbook medieval castle, then Bodiam with its symmetrical walls and towers surrounded by a moat is surely it. Built with royal permission in 1385 by Sir Edward Dalyngrigge supposedly to fend off a possible French invasion, Bodiam says more about the image Dalyngrigge wanted to project. By the sixteenth century Bodiam, besieged twice in the Wars of the Roses, was abandoned. It survives in remarkably good condition following some restoration work in the early twentieth century.

PEVENSEY CASTLE
East Sussex

Pevensey was once the Roman coastal fort of Anderida, built in the late third century. Most of the visible ruins are Roman and it was here that William the Conqueror landed in 1066. A Norman motte was raised, using the Roman fort as its bailey. A stone keep followed in the twelfth century, and a curtain wall with towers in the thirteenth. A gun was set up at Pevensey when the Spanish Armada threatened in 1588, and more gun emplacements followed in 1940.

HERSTMONCEUX CASTLE
East Sussex

Unusually, Herstmonceux was built in brick in 1441 by Sir Roger Fiennes, who used a lake as the moat. By the time Herstmonceux was built, comfort and status were more important than defence. By the late 1700s much of the castle had been robbed for building materials but in the twentieth century Herstmonceux was restored, becoming home from 1946–90 to the Royal Observatory, which needed to escape London's dirty air. Today it is a study centre for the Queen's University, Ontario.

LEWES CASTLE
East Sussex

Built by William de Warenne about 1069–70, Lewes has the rare distinction of having two mottes within its bailey. The keep was raised in the early 1100s and about a century later two semi-octagonal towers were built on. The keep still commands magnificent views across the Sussex landscape. A barbican was added to reinforce the gate in the 1300s. Today the castle is home to the Sussex Archaeological Society's collections, and its grounds are used for concerts, plays and other events.

ARUNDEL CASTLE
West Sussex

Towering over the surrounding town, Arundel Castle with all its palatial elegance bears little resemblance to the motte-and-bailey built by Roger de Montgomery, Earl of Arundel, in 1068 and the stone keep added in 1140. Badly damaged in the Civil War, the castle was later restored but it was Henry Howard, fifteenth Duke of Norfolk, who remodelled Arundel as a Gothic pile in the late 1800s. The castle has passed through various family branches, but is still owned by the earls of Arundel.

AMBERLEY CASTLE
West Sussex

Amberley started life as a hunting lodge built in 1103 by Ralph Luffa, Bishop of Chichester. Between 1370 and 1385 a new great hall was built and royal permission was granted to turn Amberley into a castle. The dissolution of the monasteries under Henry VIII in 1536–40 ended Amberley's time as a home for the bishops. Many people have leased or owned Amberley since, but it preserves its fourteenth-century walls, gatehouse and other features and is now a hotel.

HIGHCLERE CASTLE
Hampshire

Highclere's history begins in the eighth century when the Bishops of Winchester had their palace here. By the early nineteenth century Highclere was a classical mansion owned by the earls of Caernarvon, but it was swept away by the third Earl in 1838 when he commissioned Sir Charles Barry to redesign Highclere in the style of an Elizabethan manor house. With its imposing wings designed in bays with corner towers and angle turrets, Highclere is the largest house in Hampshire.

PORTCHESTER CASTLE
Hampshire

Portchester was a third-century Roman coastal fort and has the best-preserved Roman fortifications in Europe. Spotting their chance to build a stronghold that would control the harbour and act as a perfect base for naval operations, the Normans started building a castle in the corner in 1086. Portchester played a vital role in the Hundred Years' War against France. Portsmouth took away Porchester's importance but it was still serving as a prison, hospital and barracks in the nineteenth century.

CARISBROOKE CASTLE
Isle of Wight

William FitzOsbern, the Norman Lord of Wight, built a castle near Newport inside the Anglo-Saxon defences built to defend the island against the Vikings. The Redvers family took over Carisbrooke and added a keep, stone walls and a tower before selling it to Edward I in 1293. Carisbrooke was reinforced after the Spanish Armada, but was later used as a prison. The most famous inmate was Charles I, locked up here from 1647–48 before being tried and executed in London.

DUNSTER CASTLE
Somerset

Dunster Tor once overlooked the sea and was fortified by the Saxons as a defence against the Vikings. William the Conqueror gave Dunster to William de Mohun whose family owned the castle until 1376 when it was sold to Lady Elizabeth Luttrell. Her descendant George Luttrell redesigned Dunster as a Jacobean country home. The remaining defences were demolished after the Civil War, Dunster having withstood three sieges. From 1868–72 Dunster was remodelled again to look like a medieval castle once more.

CORFE CASTLE
Dorset

Generally considered one of England's most impressive ruins, Corfe was begun in the 1080s by the Normans to control the pass through the Purbeck Hills. Rebuilding and alterations followed, especially by King John (1199–1216) who was particularly fond of Corfe. The castle was besieged twice in the Civil War and fell the second time when Parliamentary troops entered disguised as Royalist reinforcements in 1646. The castle resisted attempts to demolish it completely afterwards, leaving the majestic remains visible today.

NUNNEY CASTLE
Somerset

Sir John Delamere built Nunney Castle in 1373, copying French castles he had seen while fighting in the Hundred Years' War, and paying for it with the ransom he had received from several French lords. With no proper defences like a drawbridge or portcullis, Nunney was just for show. The north wall was easily breached by cannon fire in the Civil War in 1645, and finally collapsed in 1910 by which time Nunney had been a picturesque ruin for centuries.

BLAISE CASTLE
Bristol

Blaise Castle House was built between 1796 and 1798 by a wealthy Bristol merchant called John Harford. But the house took its name from a mock castle or summerhouse built on top of Blaise Hill in 1766 by Thomas Farr, commanding splendid views across Bristol and on a clear day as far as South Wales. Blaise Castle was no folly though, and was lived in until the early twentieth century. Today it forms part of a 650-acre park open to the public.

DARTMOUTH CASTLE
Devon

Dartmouth Castle, built in 1388, guards the Dart estuary at its narrowest point. It was one of the first castles purpose-built to house artillery that could hurl stones at any enemy ship sailing by. A new and bigger tower was built from 1481–95 to house improved longer-range guns, and various other gun installations were added as military technology advanced. By most castle standards Dartmouth is small, consisting of a square and a round tower, and was last used for defence in the Second World War.

POWDERHAM CASTLE
Devon

Part of the original house at Powderham, built by Sir Philip Courtenay between 1390 and 1420, survives including the chapel's fifteenth-century roof but was largely remodelled in the 1700s as a Georgian country house. In the nineteenth century it was transformed again when in the 1840s Devon-born architect Charles Fowler (designer of Covent Garden) recreated Powderham as a Victorian version of a medieval castle with towers and battlements. Today Courtenay's descendants, the earls of Devon still own Powderham.

TINTAGEL CASTLE
Cornwall

Tintagel clings to a rocky headland only just connected to the mainland with an ancient history stretching back to Roman times and earlier. Lashed by Atlantic storms the bleak setting is matched by its legendary association with Celtic kings of the Dark Ages including King Arthur, in part substantiated by archaeology that found evidence of trade with the Byzantine Empire. The visible ruins belong to the thirteenth century and were built Richard, Earl of Cornwall (1209–72), King John's second son.

PENDENNIS CASTLE
Cornwall

Pendennis was built between 1540 and 1545 by Henry VIII as one of a pair of artillery bases on either side of the River Fal to defend England against attack by France and Spain. The Killigrew family provided the land and several Captains of the Castle. The invasion never came but Pendennis proved its worth in the English Civil War. Charles II sought refuge here and Pendennis held out against the Parliamentarians for six months. It was last used in the Second World War.

RESTORMEL CASTLE

Cornwall

Restormel Castle overlooks the River Fowey near Lostwithiel. The original castle, built around 1100, was made of timber. In the 1200s a new circular shell stone keep replaced it. Inside were all the castle buildings, including a kitchen and great hall. An unusual feature was piped water from a distant spring, augmenting the castle's well. Although the Black Prince lived here for a while in the 1360s Restormel soon fell into ruin though the Parliamentarians briefly occupied it in the Civil War.

ST MAWES CASTLE

Cornwall

Along with Pendennis, St Mawes was built between 1540 and 1545 by Henry VIII as one of a pair of artillery bases on either side of the River Fal to defend England against attack by France and Spain. Their cannons, sited on the solid bastions, could cover the entire estuary. That invasion never happened, and although St Mawes was captured by Parliament in 1646 during the Civil War it survives largely in its original form and was manned during the Second World War.

Scotland

Scotland's castles, above all, enjoy some of the most dramatic settings of any castles. Perched on volcanic outcrops, overlooking the magnificent coastline or standing on islands and promontories in lochs, they stand as bastions of security in a wild and impressive landscape that has seen some of the most exciting events in British history.

Unlike England's larger sprawling fortresses, Scottish castles are more often tower houses or compact complexes clinging to strategically vital but almost inaccessible places at the tops of cliffs. Many played important roles in the wars fought by the English kings Edward I, II and III in the late thirteenth and fourteenth centuries. For most Scottish castles the days of the Jacobite risings in 1715 and 1745–46 were very exciting times when they were held by Georgian government forces, or by the Jacobite rebels determined to put the descendants of the exiled king James II (1685–88) back on the throne.

For some of the castles these decisive events brought their stories to an end and they became evocative, haunting ruins. Others were restored and brought back to life, while some castles – and Balmoral is the best example – belong to a wholly new era of fine living in the Highlands.

ARDVRECK CASTLE

Sutherland

The McLeod family built Ardvreck's three-storey keep in 1590 in a magnificent setting on a rocky promontory on Loch Assynt. In 1650 during the Civil War the Royalist Marquis of Montrose sought sanctuary but was betrayed by the McLeods and imprisoned before being sent for execution in Edinburgh. His ghost is said to haunt Ardvreck. The Mackenzies captured Ardvreck in 1672, and built a new manor house nearby in 1726. Both fell into ruin after the house burned down in 1737.

DUNROBIN CASTLE

Sutherland

With round towers, conical spires and white walls Dunrobin looks like a fairytale castle perched on top of a steep slope. It is hard to believe the castle started life as a thirteenth-century keep and courtyard castle built by the Earls of Sutherland. It was Sir Charles Barry (1795–1860), architect of the Houses of Parliament, who redesigned Dunrobin as a blend of Scottish Baronial and French Renaissance styles, creating a 189-roomed house said to be the largest in the Scottish highlands.

EILEAN DONAN CASTLE

Inverness-shire

The castle, originally built by Alexander II (1214–49) in 1220 stands on a small island called Eilean Donan in Loch Duich. Robert the Bruce (1306–29) found sanctuary on Eilean Donan while fleeing from the English. The Spanish held Eilean Donan in 1719 during the Jacobite risings before it was captured and demolished by the Royal Navy. Eilean Donan was rebuilt in the early twentieth century and has appeared in several films including James Bond's *The World is Not Enough* (1999).

URQUHART CASTLE

Inverness-shire

Built on the banks of Loch Ness under Alexander II to control rebellious local clansmen, Urquhart often changed hands during Edward I's war of conquest. In 1479 the castle passed to the Grant family in an effort to tame the region. The prominent surviving tower was built by the Grants in 1545 but the castle soon fell into decay. It last saw action in 1690 when the Jacobites besieged Urquhart, which was blown up in 1692 to stop it being used again.

INVERNESS CASTLE

Inverness-shire

Once an eleventh-century royal fortress where Shakespeare placed Macbeth's murder of King Duncan, Inverness Castle saw action in the Civil War in 1645 and was strengthened in 1725. It was destroyed in 1746 by the Jacobite army of Bonnie Prince Charlie. Entirely rebuilt as a stone castle overlooking the River Ness between 1833 and 1836 Inverness Castle now houses the sheriff's court. Near the castle stands a statue of Flora MacDonald, who helped Charlie escape to Skye in 1746.

CASTLE STUART
Inverness-shire

In 1561 Mary Queen of Scots came home after the death of her husband, the Dauphin of France. She made her half-brother James Stuart Earl of Moray and gave him this land by the Moray Firth to rule Scotland as a regent from. He was murdered in 1570, and so was his son in 1592. The castle remained unfinished until 1625 but fell into ruin for 300 years. Now restored, and owned by Stuarts once again, the castle is a home and hotel.

ACHNACARRY CASTLE
Inverness-shire

Achnacarry lies near Ben Nevis and started life in the fifteenth century when a Cameron clan chief built Tor Castle here. In 1655 Sir Ewen Cameron demolished Tor and built Achnacarry. In 1746 the Camerons were amongst the defeated Jacobites at the Battle of Culloden and Achnacarry was demolished. In 1802 the Camerons paid a huge fine to recover the estate and built a Scottish Baronial manor house. In the Second World War Achnacarry was used by the British army for commando training.

CAWDOR CASTLE

Inverness-shire

A classic Scottish fortified tower house, Cawdor was in existence at least by 1454 when William, Thane of Cawdor, lived here and possibly as early as the 1380s. It was built around a holly tree known now to have died in 1372, but various other buildings were added in the seventeenth and nineteenth centuries. Today Cawdor is still lived in by the Cawdor family and is best known for its glorious gardens including the seventeenth-century Walled Garden and the eighteenth-century Flower Garden.

CRAIGIEVAR CASTLE

Aberdeenshire

A wealthy merchant from Aberdeen called William Forbes built Craigievar between 1610 and 1626. Known as 'Danzig Willy' for his trading success on the northern Europe sea routes, his descendants owned Craigievar until the 1960s. Designed as a Scottish Baronial-style L-shaped tower house, its distinctive features are the pink stone and the turrets, chimneys and decorative stonework clustering around the top three of its seven storeys. Many family possessions remain and the castle is owned by the National Trust of Scotland.

DUNNOTTAR CASTLE

Aberdeenshire

Dunnottar's strategic location on a rocky outcrop of Scotland's northeast coast overlooking the North Sea 50 m (164 ft) below means the site has been defended for nearly 2,000 years at least. The earliest ruins visible today date from the 1200s. Mary Queen of Scots stayed here twice in the 1560s. The Earls Marischal remodelled Dunnottar as a luxurious castle but it was badly damaged in the English Civil War. Used by the Jacobites in the 1715 rising, it was largely demolished in 1718.

CRATHES CASTLE

Aberdeenshire

BALMORAL CASTLE

Aberdeenshire

Crathes is an L-shaped tower house built between 1553 and 1596 by the Burnett of Leys family on land given to them by Robert the Bruce in 1323. Until Crathes was built the Burnetts lived in a timber fortress on an island in the Loch of Leys. A modern wing was built onto the house, replacing an eighteenth-century extension that burned down in 1966. Crathes is famous for its Jacobean painted ceilings, a top storey consisting entirely of one large gallery, and gardens.

Queen Victoria's beloved Scottish retreat, called by her 'my dear paradise in the Highlands', started life as a house built by Sir William Drummond in 1390. Queen Victoria and Prince Albert rented Balmoral in 1848, fell in love with the surroundings and decided to buy it in 1852. Albert promptly built a new house, the present castle, and turned the surrounding land into a proper working estate. The work was finished by 1856. Today Queen Elizabeth stays here every year.

INVERARAY CASTLE
Argyll

Elegantly symmetrical in the Scottish Baronial style with its four round corner towers and spires, Inverary was designed with Gothic and Palladian features for the dukes of Argyll by Sir John Vanbrugh in 1720. Work began in 1746 once the village of Inverary had been demolished to make way for it, and lasted until 1789. Surviving two serious fires in 1877 and 1975 the castle is famous for its French-painted State Dining Room and its Armoury Hall with a 21-m (69-ft) high ceiling.

CASTLE STALKER
Argyll

Castle Stalker was probably built in the mid-fifteenth century by Sir John Stewart, Lord of Lorn. The tower house is precariously perched on a tiny island in Loch Laich on the west coast of Scotland north of Oban. The castle often changed hands between the Stewart and Campbell clans. Held by the Campbells in 1745 it resisted attack by the Jacobite Stuarts. In 1840 the castle was allowed to fall into ruin but in 1908 the Stewarts purchased and restored it.

KILCHURN CASTLE

A courtyard castle on a peninsular jutting out into Loch
Awe, only accessible by water, Kilchurn has been a splendid
ruin since it was struck by lightning in 1769. It was Colin
Campbell, Lord of Glenorchy, who built Kilchurn's tower
in the 1400s. His descendant John Campbell, Earl of
Breadalbane (1635–1716), architect of the 1692 Glencoe
massacre, finished the castle by adding corner towers,
barracks, and raising the walls. During the 1715 and 1745
Jacobite risings, British government troops held Kilchurn.

STIRLING CASTLE

Stirlingshire

Alexander I (1107–24) built Stirling to oversee the strategic Forth crossing. Clamped to the top of a volcanic crag with cliffs on three sides, Stirling was lost to the English twice. The Battles of Stirling Bridge in 1297 and Bannockburn in 1314 were fought to win it back. James III (1460–88), James IV (1488–1513) and James V (1513–42) completely rebuilt Stirling including the Great Parliament Hall. The young James VI, England's James I (1603–25), grew up here.

EDINBURGH CASTLE

Edinburgh

Sitting astride the basalt remains of an extinct volcano, Edinburgh Castle has one of the most striking of all Scottish castle settings. Approached from the Esplanade that joins the Royal Mile stretching through the New Town of Edinburgh from Holyrood Palace, the oldest surviving part is the twelfth-century St Margaret's chapel. One of the most prominent features is the 1574 drum-shaped Half Moon battery. The castle is still the British army's Scottish headquarters, and houses the Scottish crown jewels.

TANTALLON CASTLE
East Lothian

Tantallon is largely protected by cliffs and the Firth of Forth and overlooks the Bass Rock, but on its landward side the massive 15-m (50-ft) high curtain wall is its most impressive feature. Built by the Douglas family in the mid-1300s who divided into the rival Black and Red Douglases, Tantallon was used to resist the crown. In 1528 James V laid siege and seriously damaged Tantallon. The castle was strengthened but in 1651 fell to the Parliamentarian army of Oliver Cromwell.

BOTHWELL CASTLE
Strathclyde

Bothwell Castle guards a bend in the River Clyde. The cylindrical keep was built in the thirteenth century by Walter of Moray but was wrecked during the war with Edward I of England. Edward took Bothwell in 1296 but after a 14-month siege the Scots won it back. Bothwell changed hands several times thereafter. The castle was massively enlarged in the 1400s. Various owners followed until 1700 when the earls of Forfar abandoned Bothwell but the surviving remains are extremely impressive.

CAERLAVEROCK CASTLE
Dumfries & Galloway

Lying by the Solway Firth in marshland and surrounded by a double moat, no other castle shares Caerlaverock's unusual triangular plan with a gatehouse at the apex. No one really knows who built Caerlaverock but Edward I seized it in 1300. In 1312 it was recaptured and demolished. It was later rebuilt and turned into a more comfortable home by the Earl of Nithsdale in the 1630s who added a sophisticated classical apartment block. Caerlaverock was wrecked during the Civil War.

Wales

Wales has been the setting of warfare since ancient times. The Romans spent decades trying to conquer the tribes. The Normans moved rapidly into Wales, building castles such as Chepstow to control key routes.

Various lords built their own castles and the most remarkable of these must be Caerphilly, which is the biggest in Wales and one of the most impressively well-preserved. It is ironic that Caerphilly was a private enterprise, built as the result of a feud between two Welsh barons, because the main story in Welsh castle-building came only a few years later when Edward I of England decided to conquer Wales once and for all.

The first war lasted from 1276 to 1277 but a rebellion by Llewellyn in 1282 led to a new war that Edward followed with a massive programme of castle building. This resulted in some of Europe's most magnificent castles, mainly designed by Edward's architect James of St George who left us the imposing remains at Beaumaris, Harlech and Caernarfon amongst others. As so often with British castles, the last act for many came with the Civil War but Cardiff's remodelling and rebuilt Roman walls brings the story of Welsh castles right up to modern times.

BEAUMARIS CASTLE

Anglesey

Beaumaris is French for the 'beautiful marsh'. Started in 1295, it was the last in Edward I's programme of castle-building in Wales. Designed by Edward's military architect, James of St George, Beaumaris was planned as a symmetrical structure contained within a concentric outer ward and had a defended dock. By 1298 Edward was fighting in Scotland and money ran out. Work was restarted in 1306 but in 1330 Beaumaris was abandoned half-finished, leaving it a textbook example of castle-building work in progress.

CAERNARFON CASTLE

Gwynedd

Generally considered to be Edward I's finest Welsh castle, Caernarfon was begun in 1283 after the Llewellyn uprising. Work carried on until 1323 though even then it was unfinished and remains more or less in that state today. Its magnificent and sophisticated battlements with bands of different coloured stone, reputedly modelled by Edward on the walls of Constantinople, dominate Caernarfon today. The first modern investiture of a Prince of Wales took place here in 1911, and the tradition has continued since.

HARLECH CASTLE
Gwynedd

Harlech was built on top of a coastal cliff between 1283 and 1290 by Edward I to hold Snowdonia. Protected on the landward side by a moat and huge fortified gateway, Harlech was still captured by Owain Glyndwr in 1404 but Henry V recaptured it. Harlech had a steep staircase down the cliff so that it could be supplied by sea. This way it held out for seven years for the Lancastrians in the Wars of the Roses until 1468.

CONWY CASTLE
Gwynedd

Built between 1283 and 1289 by Edward I to control the Conwy estuary and the medieval walled town, Conwy has a long thin layout to fit on the rocky outcrop. Eight massive round towers in the walls surrounding the adjacent inner and outer wards protected the garrison and barbicans reinforced the entrances at either end. Conwy soon fell into disuse apart from a brief revival during the Civil War in the 1640s but remains one of Britain's most impressive castles.

POWYS CASTLE
Powys

Unlike so many Welsh medieval castles, Powys Castle has remained in use. Today the home of the Earl of Powys, it is famous for its gardens. Little is known of its origins but in 1578 Sir Edward Herbert acquired Powys and restored it. Captured by Parliament in 1644 during the Civil War and garrisoned, Powys had to be restored once again but more in the style of an elegant country home. More renovations followed in the eighteenth and nineteenth centuries.

CAREW CASTLE
Pembrokeshire

Carew's history goes back at least to the twelfth century, but Sir Nicholas Carew rebuilt the castle in the late thirteenth century, adding a great hall and towers. Rhys ap Thomas bought it in 1480. He supported Henry Tudor, was rewarded with honours and jobs when Henry became king, and substantially improved the castle. Thanks to later treacherous Carews the castle changed hands until it was bought back in 1607. It fell into ruin when the Carews moved to Somerset in 1686.

PEMBROKE CASTLE
Pembrokeshire

In 1199 William Marshal, Earl of Pembroke, created a massive circular stone keep at Pembroke. His sons and later owners completed the castle's other buildings but Pembroke fell into decline until the Tudor family acquired it. The future Henry VII was born here in 1457. During the Civil War Pembroke was Parliamentarian but Cromwell had to besiege some of his own troops in the castle who had declared for Charles I. Demolition followed but Pembroke was restored in the twentieth century.

LAUGHARNE CASTLE
Camarthenshire

Laugharne stood guard over a violent and dangerous place from the twelfth century onwards. In the thirteenth century the de Brian family began the stone castle. In 1575 Sir John Perrot was given Laugharne by Elizabeth I but when he was put into prison for treason, looters stripped the castle of anything they could carry away. Royalists held out here in the Civil War but the Parliamentarians destroyed the defences. In the eighteenth century Laugharne was landscaped as a romantic ruin.

OYSTERMOUTH CASTLE
Swansea

A particularly attractive ruin overlooking Swansea Bay near Mumbles, some of the visible remains at Oystermouth date back to the twelfth century, though most is thirteenth century when the de Braos family were the lords of Gower. A chapel block, much of which survives, was added in the fourteenth century though Oystermouth had already started falling into ruin by the sixteenth century. But with its overgrown walls and delicately carved windows, Oystermouth is one of Wales's most romantic monuments.

WEOBLY CASTLE

Swansea

CAERPHILLY CASTLE

Mid Glamorgan

Weobly was built as a fortified manor house by the de la Bere family during the fourteenth century on the Gower peninsula overlooking the Llanrhidian salt marsh across the Loughor estuary from Llanelli. The de la Beres worked as stewards to the de Braos lords of Gower. Four wings surround a small courtyard, and boast latrines, a banqueting hall and an oak screen. Rhys ap Thomas, an ally of Henry VII's, acquired Weobly in the late 1400s and added a two-storey porch.

Caerphilly is a monument to Gilbert 'the Red' de Clare's feud with Llewellyn. Begun by Gilbert in 1268, its 30-acre (12-hectare) concentric design makes it the largest in Wales and the second largest in Britain. No one knows how long it took to complete but the result was a magnificent castle with lakes on either side, an additional fortified compound and a huge fortified platform with bastions to the east. Disused by the late fifteenth century, Caerphilly was damaged in the Civil War.

CASTELL COCH

South Glamorgan

The present Castell Coch (Red Castle in Welsh) began life as an eleventh century earth and timber motte castle, and after a courtyard and towers were added during Norman times it was abandoned in the early fourteenth century. In the 1870s, architect William Burges began restoring the ruin on behalf of the third Marquess of Bute. This fairytale construction was completed in the 1890s, and although the exterior may appear authentic, Castell Coch is a true romantic folly, with a richly decorated interior.

CARDIFF CASTLE

Cardiff

Cardiff has the most curious mix of periods. The original Roman fort was buried by the Normans who built a twelfth-century keep. Further walls, towers and a gatehouse followed. By the mid-eighteenth century the castle was ruinous. Some parts were demolished in the 1770s and the moat filled in to create a landscaped home for the Marquesses of Bute. In 1869 Cardiff was designed as a Gothic castle, but in the 1920s the Roman walls were completely rebuilt on the ancient foundations.

CHEPSTOW CASTLE

Monmouthshire

One of Britain's earliest Norman castles, Chepstow was begun in 1067 by William FitzOsbern to control the route from England into Wales across the River Wye. The castle with its three baileys and massive walls stretches along the top of a sheer drop down into the river on the edge of the modern town and forms a magnificent backdrop. Although it fell twice to Parliament in the Civil War, Chepstow was kept in commission until 1690 when it fell into ruin.

RAGLAN CASTLE

Monmouthshire

The original Raglan Castle was a Norman motte and bailey. It was acquired in the fifteenth century by the Welsh knight Sir William ap Thomas. He was responsible for the construction of its hexagonal keep. During the Civil War it was held for the king, and came under attack in 1646 by Thomas Fairfax. It withstood the war's longest siege before surrendering. Partly destroyed by the victorious Parliamentarians, it was further ransacked by the Duke of Beaufort for fittings for his new home at Badminton, leaving it derelict.

Ireland

Ireland's beautiful landscape of rolling green hills, fields, rivers and loughs belies its turbulent history.

Before the time of the Anglo-Normans, the Irish chieftain clans and Vikings had long been involved in fighting territorial wars. The arrival of Richard de Clare, second Earl of Pembroke known as 'Strongbow' (1130–76) to help Diarmait Mac Murchada, the ousted king of Leinster recover his throne in one of those wars, changed everything. The Anglo-Norman conquest of Ireland followed and linked Ireland inextricably to what happened in England over the succeeding years.

Castles like Trim were built to enforce Anglo-Norman control of Ireland. The Irish clans built their own tower castles, like the MacNamaras' Bunratty Castle. Bunratty's violent history, seeing four castles succeed one after the other on the same site, symbolizes the instability that characterizes Irish medieval history. As English control tightened under Elizabeth I and then Cromwell rebellion was inevitable. Many Irish castles were damaged or destroyed in the war of 1641–53 against English rule, and others saw action when the exiled Catholic King James II fought against William III in 1690. Many lie in ruins now, while others are restored, but Dublin Castle above all has played a part in every part of this history to the present time.

DONEGAL CASTLE
Co. Donegal

Donegal's name comes from Dún na nGall which means 'fort of the foreigner', perhaps harking back to a Viking fort. The fortified manor house was begun by Hugh Roe O'Donnell, from one of Ireland's most powerful families, by the Eske river. An Englishman called Henry Sydney said in 1566 it was 'the greatest I ever saw in an Irishman's hands'. The English Brooke family acquired Donegal in 1611 but it was in ruins by the eighteenth century. It has now been largely restored.

AUGHNANURE CASTLE
Co. Galway

Aughnanure, from Achadh na nIubhar meaning 'field of yews', is a well-preserved tower house built close to Lough Corrib on a virtual island in the Drimmeen river around 1500 by the O'Flaherty family. Known as the 'ferocious O'Flaherties' the family was one of the most powerful. The tower has six storeys and stood beside two fortified courtyards (bawns) with a banqueting hall. Aughnanure came under English control in the late 1500s but the O'Flaherties managed to recover ownership until the 1950s.

BUNRATTY CASTLE
Co. Clare

The present Bunratty Castle, now Ireland's most accurately and completely restored castles, was built in 1425 by the MacNamaras, following three earlier castles which were all destroyed in warfare. In 1475 Bunratty was taken over by the immensely powerful and wealthy O'Brien family who submitted to Henry VIII. In Cromwell's time the O'Briens left and Bunratty was given to Protestant Plantation families. In 1804 the last family, the Studdarts, left and Bunratty fell into ruin until restoration started after 1945.

ROSS CASTLE
Co. Kerry

Built in the fifteenth century next to Lough Leane by a member of the O'Donoghue clan, Ross Castle is a tower house with overhanging corner turrets (bartizans) and a bawn fortified with towers, though much of the bawn was removed in the eighteenth century. In 1652 Ross Castle was the last Catholic-held castle to surrender to Cromwell's army during the war that started with the rebellion of 1641, and only fell when it was bombarded from the lough as well.

BLARNEY CASTLE
Co. Cork

Blarney's imposing tower house castle was built by Dermot McCarthy, King of Munster, in 1446 over the remains of an older stone castle dating to 1210. The castle's most famous feature is the Blarney Stone, reputed to endow anyone who kisses it with eloquence. The Protestant Jeffryes family acquired Blarney after William III's war against the deposed Catholic king James II in 1690. They added a Georgian Gothic house beside the keep, followed by a new castle nearby in 1874.

CAHIR CASTLE
Co. Tipperary

It was Conor O'Brien, Prince of Thomond, who began Cahir Castle on an island in the River Suir in 1142. Cahir became one of Ireland's largest castles. In 1375 the Butlers, barons of Cahir, were given Cahir for loyalty to Edward III, but changed sides during a rebellion against English rule in 1599. The Earl of Essex took Cahir after a short siege. More sieges followed in the war of 1641–53 but Cahir fell in 1650. The castle is extremely well-preserved.

LISMORE CASTLE
Co. Waterford

Lismore enjoys spectacular panoramic views across the Blackwater valley to the Knockmealdown Mountains. Once lived in by Sir Walter Raleigh it passed to the earls of Cork and from them by marriage to the dukes of Devonshire in 1753 who still own Lismore today. Now with magnificent interiors including a banqueting hall designed by Augustus Pugin, and a seventeenth-century garden, the castle's history stretches all the way back to the late twelfth century when it was built by King John.

KILKENNY CASTLE
Co. Kilkenny

In 1967 the Marquess of Ormonde, whose Butler family ancestors acquired Kilkenny in 1391, sold it to Ireland's Castle Restoration Committee for a nominal £50. Now fully restored, Kilkenny preserves three towers from the original trapezoidal stone castle built in 1207 by William Marshall, Earl of Pembroke, and nephew of the great Anglo-Norman warrior Richard de Clare 'Strongbow' who built a wooden castle here in 1172. Kilkenny was badly damaged in a Cromwellian assault of 1650, but it was later rebuilt.

DUBLIN CASTLE
Co. Dublin

Dublin Castle is now a major state building complex that has been used for government ceremonies since 1922 but its history dates back to a castle built between 1204 and 1230 on King John's orders. Serving as the headquarters of British rule, Dublin Castle became a hated symbol. It was destroyed by fire in 1684, possibly deliberately, but was soon rebuilt. Not until 1922 was the Castle handed over to the Irish Free State after the War of Independence that started in 1919.

TRIM CASTLE
Co. Meath

Trim's unique cruciform keep was built by Hugh de Lacy and Walter de Lacy between 1174 and 1206 to act as the centre of government for Meath, on a site that overlooks a ford on the River Boyne. Trim served the role for around 200 years and became one of Europe's largest castles. It declined in importance and after the war with Cromwell between 1641 and 1653 it was given to the future Duke of Wellington's family but is now owned by the state.

FERNS CASTLE
Co. Wexford

Ferns dates back to the 1200s and may have been built by William Marshal, Earl of Pembroke (d. 1219), regent of England under King John and owner of extensive lands in Ireland. The castle was built in square form on high ground in the middle of Ferns with corner towers, using stone cut out of the castle moat. Around half the structure has collapsed leaving two impressive towers with the remains of an ornately decorated chapel and some of the walls.

Western Europe

The amazing variety of castles in Western Europe is summed up by the contrast between the water lapping around the Belém Tower in the River Tagus near Lisbon and the Castelbello high above the Venosta valley in northern Italy.

The settings reflect the enormous variety of landscapes in Europe and the need to defend everything from river estuaries to mountain passes. Ever since the Western Roman Empire collapsed in the fifth century, Western Europe fragmented into an almost infinite variety of kingships, dukedoms, principalities and the papal states. The result is a quite extraordinary range of castle designs. Some of Spain and Portugal's castles date back to the days when Islam controlled most of the Iberian peninsular and to the wars that followed between the Moors and Christians.

France's sophistication from the fifteenth century on saw many medieval castles replaced by extravagant chateaux such as Chenonceau. The story of the Castel Nuovo at Naples is a reminder that this was an age of almost continuous warfare in the struggle to conquer more territory. So Frederick II's Castel del Monte is all the more remarkable as an example of the culture, education and science that survived the chaos and paved the way for modern Europe.

SILVES CASTLE
Algarve, Portugal

Silves Castle is a massive structure on a hill overlooking Silves and dates back to the Moorish occupation of the Iberian peninsula. It changed hands frequently during the struggle by combined forces of crusaders to eject the Moors until finally it was seized for Portugal in 1242. Alfonso III (1248–79) restored the sprawling complex with its 11 square towers, two barbicans and two gates. Earthquakes in 1722 and 1755 caused more damage, but the castle was restored again in 1940.

BELÉM TOWER
Lisbon, Portugal

Belém Tower is a five-storey fortified lighthouse, built between 1515 and 1521 to defend the port at Belém. It was designed in the Manueline style, and was a starting point for sixteenth- and seventeenth-century explorers. Its exterior features rope carved in stone, openwork balconies, Moorish-style watchtowers and distinctive battlements in the shape of shields. The tower has been used as a prison. French troops destroyed its top two storeys in 1807, which were later rebuilt. The tower has a whispering gallery and spectacular views.

ALCÁZAR CASTLE
Segovi, Spain

Alcázar comes from the Moorish word for 'castle'. Alcázar was built during the Moorish occupation of Spain but the remodelling by Alfonso XI in 1327 including Moorish-style baths and tall round towers with their conical spires, created one of the most beautiful castles in Europe. Alcázar was badly damaged by fire in 1862. Now restored as a museum with extensive gardens Alcázar is sometimes known as the 'ship castle' thanks to its prow-like barbican and setting on a huge rocky outcrop.

PEÑAFIEL CASTLE
Valladolid, Spain

Unusually long and narrow – the castle is 210 m (690 ft) long but only 33 m (108 ft) wide – Peñafiel Castle's history stretches back to the tenth century. Lying on the border with Moslem Spain, Peñafiel played an important role in the wars between the Moors and Christians as well as the squabbles between Christian rulers and rebels. Destroyed after a rebellion was started here in 1341, Peñafiel was rebuilt in 1456 by Don Pedro Girón, preserving the prominent late-thirteenth-century central tower.

CASTLE OF KNIGHTS TEMPLAR

Ponferrada, Leon, Spain

Ponferrada was begun in 1178 by the monastic soldiers of the Knights Templar to protect pilgrims on their way to walk the Way of St James to the cathedral of Santiago de Compostela. The Knights were dissolved in 1312 and the castle passed to new owners who improved the defences by adding towers and a new keep. The castle survived until 1811 when it was partly demolished to prevent the French from using it during the Peninsular War of 1808–14.

VINCENNES CASTLE
Île de France, France

The Chateau de Vincennes is now so enormous a French royal palace, it is difficult to believe it was once a modest hunting lodge built in 1150 by Louis VII. Philip VI Valois added a colossal 52-m (170-ft) high keep in 1337, and by 1410 Vincennes had a 1-km (⅔-mile) long curtain wall with towers. More wings were added by Louis XIV (1643–1715) but when Versailles drained resources Vincennes was abandoned and later became porcelain and armaments factories, a prison and Nazi headquarters.

TARASCON CASTLE
Provence, France

Tarascon is an imposingly monolithic looking castle with sheer white walls and decorative battlements. Begun in its present form by Louis II of Anjou (1384–1417) beside the Rhône to guard Provence, the castle was completed by his second son René I of Naples in 1449, and is usually known as 'René's Castle'. Its austere exterior gives little idea of the interior decoration though it was used as a prison from the seventeenth century until it became a museum in the 1930s.

AVIGNON CASTLE
Provence, France

Chaos in Rome led Pope Clement V to remove the papacy to Avignon, owned by the King of Sicily. Staying until 1377, the popes lived in the extravagant Palais de Papes, constructed between 1334 and 1352. Although built in Gothic style with enormous walls around 4 m (13 ft) thick on an impregnable rocky outcrop, the popes lived here in such luxury and comfort that it caused outrage amongst an impoverished population. Later used as a barracks, the castle is now a museum.

FOIX CASTLE
Pyrenees, France

Built in dangerous bandit territory to control movement through the Ariège river valley, the castle is superbly located on an almost impregnable rock. Dominated today by its three enormous towers, each a different shape and size, Ariège was lived in by the counts of Foix from the eleventh century. It fell once, in 1272, to King Philip the Bold, when home to the Albigensian heretics. By the seventeenth century it was used by governors of the region and served as a prison.

CHÂTEAU DE CHENONCEAU

Loire Valley, France

Chenonceau sits on arches across the River Cher, a tributary of the Loire. It was built by Thomas Bohier in 1513 but it was his wife Catherine who oversaw most of the construction. After their deaths it passed to the crown and Henry II (1547–59) gave it to his favourite Diane de Poitiers. She added a bridge but after Henry died his queen Catherine de'Medici demanded it back and added a gallery over the bridge, creating Chenonceau's most famous feature. Chenonceau is now often called 'Château of the Ladies' because of the women in its history.

CHÂTEAU DE CHAUMONT
Loire Valley, France

Perched on a hillside on the banks of the Loire and commanding exceptional views, Chaumont dwarfs the village houses immediately below. Charles d'Amboise began Chaumont in 1466, replacing an old feudal medieval fortress destroyed by Louis XI (1461–83). In 1559 Queen Catherine de'Medici bought Chaumont but then demanded a swap with her husband's mistress Diane de Poitiers and moved to Chenonceau. Today the château preserves its drawbridge and a huge collection of sixteenth- and seventeenth-century tapestries.

CHÂTEAU DE CHAMBORD

Loire Valley, France

Chambord is a royal French chateau begun by Francis I in 1519, but building work (which sometimes involved up to 2,000 men) lasted through several reigns until that of Henry III (1574–89). Ironically, it was never much used even though one story is that Leonardo da Vinci had helped design the château. With its unique double staircase, and extraordinary façade with large circular towers, conical spires with cupolas, and a cluster of chimneys, Chambord is the largest of the Loire Valley chateaux.

CHÂTEAU D'USSE
Loire Valley, France

Begun in 1462 by Jean de Beuil, D'Usse, said by some to be the inspiration for the story of the 'Sleeping Beauty' by Charles Perrault, lies between the Loire and the Forest of Chinon. Part of the château was demolished in the seventeenth century to open up the courtyard to a view down across formal gardens to the Loire. The layout is asymmetrical with one much larger tower overlooking the rest. Never a royal palace, d'Usse is still privately owned.

CASTEL DEL MONTE
Andria, Italy

The Holy Roman Emperor Frederick II (1220–50) built the Castel del Monte during his war against the popes and the Lombard League. Highly educated he was fascinated by all different cultures and designed the castle as a blend of Classical, Islamic and Gothic styles with a perfectly symmetrical octagonal keep with an octagonal tower at each corner and an octagonal interior, mathematically orientated to act as a sundial and observatory. Although abandoned after his death, the castle is largely intact.

CASTELBELLO
Bolzano, Italy

Defying gravity, Castelbello (also known as Kastelbell) teeters on a rock overlooking the stunning Venosta valley. It was built in 1238 by the lord of Montalban but in 1577 it was pawned by the Holy Roman Emperor to the Hendl family. In 1826 a serious fire started a long period of decay but repair work started in 1956. Today the castle is fully restored, including a chapel with fourteenth-century frescoes, and contains an exhibition about the Roman road through the valley.

CASTEL NUOVO
Naples, Italy

A stunningly imposing castle with enormous round towers and battlements, the 'New Castle' was built between 1279 and 1282 for Charles I, King of Naples and Count of Anjou. Generally considered a Renaissance masterpiece of military architecture, the castle's entrance boasts the triumphal arch of Alfonso I of Aragon commemorating his expulsion of the Angevins in 1442 when he captured Naples. By then the castle was in ruins but was completely rebuilt by the new Aragon rulers. Today the castle is a museum.

Central Europe

In political terms medieval central Europe bears no resemblance at all to the way it is today. The dominant power was the Holy Roman Empire made up of numerous elector princes but the situation was in constant flux.

It is no wonder then that the castles of the region show such extraordinary variation over such a long period. Belgium's Beersel Castle was badly damaged in a rebellion against the Holy Roman Empire, while Salzburg's castle has survived more than 900 years without being attacked.

The most remarkable type of castle found in central Europe is the romantic revivalist castle. Ludwig II of Bavaria's vast Neuschwanstein is a monument to his fantasies of medieval splendour, while the much less imposing Anif Castle in Austria was recreated in a similar style and found itself playing a role in the world's most famous musical movie. Other older castles in Germany were built for harshly practical reasons like defence and also to tax the lucrative trade that flowed up and down the River Rhine. But few of the older castles illustrated here bear any resemblance to how they were built. Most have been restored. Ghent's Gravensteen with its huge surviving twelfth-century keep is a rare example of a castle in its original form.

MONTEBELLO CASTLE
Bellinzona, Switzerland

Montebello is just one of three castles protecting Bellinzona, a strategically important city where several Alpine passes meet. It was built around 1300 but was later joined up to Bellinzona's walls. By the fifteenth century it had fallen into decay but in 1462 renovation and extension work started and this is the form it survives in today. The castle is diamond-shaped with several towers, looks out over steep terraces of vineyards, and is now home to the local history and archaeology museum.

CHÂTEAU DE CHILLON
Lake Geneva, Switzerland

Built on a rocky island by Lake Geneva, Chillon guarded the ancient road through the St Bernard Pass from Switzerland into Italy. The castle is now a complex of buildings from different periods dating back 1,000 years. The main work took place when Peter II of Savoy (1263–68) rebuilt the castle. By the sixteenth century Chillon was used as a prison where François Bonivard (1496–1570), a Swiss patriot was locked up. This inspired Byron's 1816 poem 'The Prisoner of Chillon'.

SALZBURG CASTLE
Salzburg, Austria

Said to be Europe's best-preserved castle Salzburg has never been attacked, despite dating back to 1077 when it was begun by Archbishop Gebhard. During the Peasants' Revolt of 1525–26 the castle was besieged but escaped damage. In the fifteenth and sixteenth centuries the castle was greatly enlarged, and a granary and arsenal installed. In the late 1600s Italian Baroque decoration was added. The castle overlooks Salzburg, ruled by its archbishop until 1803, from its 120-m (394-ft) high hill called the Mönchsberg.

ANIF CASTLE
Salzburg, Austria

Anif lies south of Salzburg and was once the home of the bishops of Chiemseehof, named after Lake Chiemsee in Bavaria. A place of no architectural consequence in the middle of the lake until the nineteenth century when, after Count Arco-Stebburg bought it, Anif was completely remodelled as a neo-Gothic castle between 1838 and 1848 with a prominent single tower and hall. The building is famous today as the castle appearing at the beginning of *The Sound of Music* filmed in 1965.

TRATZBERG CASTLE
Stans, Austria

Today Tratzberg is a white-walled palace with thin round towers on a steep hill on the Bavarian border, and replaced an earlier medieval fortress nearby. Built in 1500, Tratzberg was used by the Emperor Maximilian (1493–1519) as a hunting lodge. Owned by the Enzenberg family since 1848, the castle and its Renaissance interiors, including the Queen's Chamber, have been preserved in excellent condition. The most unusual feature is the Hapsburg Room with 148 portraits depicting the Hapsburg family tree.

HOCHOSTERWITZ
Carinthia, Austria

One of the oldest Austrian castles, Hochosterwitz dates back to around AD 860 and sits on top of an extraordinary pinnacle of rock in the middle of a valley plain. Hochosterwitz fell to the Emperor Frederick III in 1475. By 1571 it had been bought by Baron George of Khevenhüller whose family still own it. He added 14 fortified gates and built a winding trackway through them up to the castle that exposed any attackers to missiles hurled down by the defenders.

FALKENSTEIN

Hettstedt, Germany

Falkenstein's most remarkable feature is the sequence of six heavily defended gates into the castle. Originally built in the early 1100s and lived in by the counts of Falkenstein ('falcon stone') the castle was enlarged substantially in the fifteenth century and survived occupation by troops in the Thirty Years' War (1618–48). Abandoned as a home in the eighteenth century the castle was restored in 1826 but at the end of the First World War was used by resistance fighters against the Allied advance.

PFALZGRAFENSTEIN
Bavaria, Germany

Pfalzgrafenstein ('duke's palace on a rock') was built on a rocky island in the middle of the Rhine in 1327 by Duke Ludwig IV of Bavaria, and strengthened in 1338. The castle's job was to levy customs duties on traffic passing along the river. With its pier-shaped outer walls to resist the river and a substantial central tower the castle resembles a stout ship. The surviving castle is mostly fourteenth century and now serves as a museum of seventeenth- to nineteenth-century ceramics.

NEUSCHWANSTEIN
Bavaria, Germany

Neuschwanstein is Germany's most famous fortress thanks to its spectacular design as the ultimate fairytale castle with soaring white gables and towers. Ludwig II, King of Bavaria (1864–86), had a mania for Wagner's music and fantasy castles. Neuschwanstein was built between 1869 and 1886 looking over Lake Alpsee below the Alps and features murals depicting scenes from Wagner's operas. Considering that Ludwig's own bedroom took more than four years to complete it is not surprising that Neuschwanstein remains about two-thirds unfinished.

HOHENSCHWANGAU
Bavaria, Germany

Hohenschwangau ('hilltop land of swans') is the older of the two castles near Füssen, the other being Ludwig II's Neuschwanstein. Hohenschwangau was built between 1538 and 1547 on the site of the twelfth-century fortress of Schwanstein but it had fallen into ruins by the early 1800s. The Crown Prince Maximilian (King of Bavaria from 1825 to 1848 and father of Ludwig II) bought the site in 1832 and rebuilt it to the original design to serve as his main summer and hunting residence.

GLUECKSBURG
Flensburg, Germany

When originally built by Duke Johann the Younger of Schleswig-Holstein in the 1580s, the French-style Gluecksburg looked more like a castle with battlements on its corner towers. Built on granite foundations sunk into an artificial lake Gluecksburg was lived in by the dukes until Frederick VII of Denmark (1848–63) took it over and remodelled it. Prussian soldiers used the castle during the war of 1863–66 over control of Schleswig-Holstein. Christian IX (1863–1906), ancestor of the Duke of Edinburgh, lived here.

STAHLECK

Rhine Valley, Germany

Stahleck clings to the hillside above Bacharach overlooking the River Rhine. It dates back to the twelfth century when the archbishops of Cologne built the castle to guard a valley intersection. Later it was used to collect customs duties from river traffic. Blown up by French troops in 1689 during the War of the League of Augsburg (1689–98) Stahleck was in ruins until 1925 when it was rebuilt as a youth hostel, and later used to indoctrinate young people by the Nazis.

RHEINSTEIN

Rhine Valley, Germany

Rheinstein ('Rhine rock') dates back more than 11 centuries to when it was built on an 83-m (272-ft) high ridge by the Rhine to enforce customs dues on river traffic. The Holy Roman Emperor Rudolph I (1273–91) lived here but from the 1300s the archbishops of Mainz leased it. It fell into ruin in the late sixteenth century but was transformed by Prince Frederick Wilhelm Ludwig of Bavaria's restoration of 1825–29 as part of the Romantic movement of the period.

KATZ

Rhine Valley, Germany

The castle is named after Count Wilhelm II von Katzenelnbogen who built it to guard St Goarshausen in the late fourteenth century. It survived the War of the League of Augsburg but was destroyed by Napoleon in 1806. Katz was rebuilt at the end of the nineteenth century in mock-Gothic style and apart from the two thin round towers with conical spires more resembles an elaborate mountain manor house. Today the castle is used as a school.

SOONECK
Rhine Valley, Germany

Sooneck's present state belongs to the 1842–61 restoration by Prince Frederick Wilhelm Ludwig of Bavaria, having been in ruins since 1689. The castle dates back to the eleventh century but it was destroyed in the late 1200s to punish its robber baron owners. The castle was rebuilt in the mid-fourteenth century and lasted until the War of the League of Augsburg of 1689–98. The nineteenth century restoration work unusually preserved much of the original castle including the prominent main tower.

JEHAY CASTLE
Liege, Belgium

Jehay is surrounded by water that enhances the curious effect of its brown-and-white chequerboard construction, in contrast to its red brick gatehouse with its extraordinary spire and weather vane. Although the Jehay seigneury dates back to the eleventh century the castle was built around 1550 by the Mérode family. By 1680 the van Steen family had bought Jehay and still own it. Badly damaged when railway workers were billeted here in the Second World War, the castle has since been restored to its original condition.

VÊVES CASTLE
Namur, Belgium

In the hands of the de Beaufort family by the twelfth century, the eighth-century castle at Vêves on the edge of the Ardennes forest burned down in 1200 and 1466 but was rebuilt both times. The family still own Vêves. Today the 36-m (118-ft) high thirteenth-century keep with its dungeon, and six conical towers is the main original part. Inside, the courtyard is overlooked by a two-storey timber gallery added in 1715, and the castle now serves as a museum of medieval and Renaissance furniture.

GRAVENSTEEN
Ghent, Belgium

Gravensteen ('the count's castle') was begun in stone by the year 1000 but followed at least three timber predecessors dating back to Count Baldwin I in AD 868. Most of the existing castle was built by Count Philip of Alsace between 1157 and 1191, and a cross in the monumental gateway commemorates his time as a crusader. His keep still towers over the city of Ghent. Later Gravensteen was used as Ghent's mint and prison. The castle is now restored as a museum.

BEERSEL CASTLE
Flemish Brabant, Belgium

Beersel was built from brick between 1300 and 1310 by Godfrey of Hellebeek. Since the site lacks natural defences Beersel had an exceptionally large moat. That did not prevent it being besieged and badly damaged in 1489 when Flanders revolted against the Holy Roman Emperor Maximilian I and rebels attacked his supporters at Beersel. Maximilian forced the rebels to rebuild Beersel. By the eighteenth century Beersel was abandoned and in 1818 was used for cotton textiles. It was restored after 1928.

MUIDERSLOT
Muiden, Netherlands

After Muiderslot (Castle of Muidin) was destroyed in 1296 the castle was completely rebuilt by Duke Albrecht of the Netherlands on a square plan with four round corner towers and surrounded by a moat. Oddly it was only ever used as a courthouse and prison though it was later incorporated into a system of earthwork and water defences for Holland. In ruins by the early 1800s Muiderslot was nearly demolished but fortunately plans changed and it was restored. Today it is Holland's most popular castle.

CASTLE DE HAAR
Haarzuilens, Netherlands

The castle was built in the late 1300s by the de Haars, who served the bishops of Utrecht. Later owned by the de Zuylen family, it was destroyed in 1482 during fighting between the bishop and Utrecht. It was rebuilt as an irregular pentagon with only three towers but after 1672 fell into ruin until a de Zuylen descendant restored it in the 1890s. The courtyard was converted into an enormous decorated hall. Outside, bartizans complete the impression of a fantasy castle.

Northern Europe

Northern Europe's history has been dominated by the sea. In the Dark Ages this was where many of the peoples who set out to conquer parts of western Europe came from.

Between the eighth and tenth centuries AD Vikings from Denmark ravaged the British Isles and other places, settling widely and even finding their way to Greenland and North America. By the twelfth century Denmark had become an important independent power in the Baltic Sea, a position it maintained. So it is no surprise to see that one of Denmark's most important castles, Kronborg, was built to control the incredibly lucrative trade from the Baltic to Western Europe.

In 1397 Sweden, Denmark and Norway were unified under a single monarch but Sweden broke away in 1449 creating new tensions. Sweden's Gripsholm Castle was the work of Gustavus I, the king who asserted Sweden's independence in the sixteenth century. Two of the most significant figures in Denmark's castle-building history were Frederick II and Christian IV. Between them they created new castles and converted old ones into fortified Renaissance palaces during the late sixteenth and early seventeenth centuries, particularly favouring Dutch architects. It was a time when Denmark repeatedly struggled unsuccessfully to recapture Sweden and also fought for a time in the destructive Thirty Years' War.

FREDERIKSBORG CASTLE
Hillerød, Denmark

Frederiksborg is named after Frederick II of Denmark who built the oldest parts around 1560. But it was his son Christian IV (1588–1648) who was responsible for the castle's present appearance. Stunningly sited on three islands in the middle of Slotsø ('Palace') Lake, Frederiksborg remained in use for Danish royal ceremonial events and survived a serious fire in 1859, being fully restored afterwards. The chapel now serves as the local parish church, and the castle is Denmark's National History Museum.

ROSENBORG CASTLE

Copenhagen, Denmark

Rosenborg has been a museum since 1838 but was built just outside Copenhagen's defences by Christian IV (1588–1648). He used it as a summer residence and retreat from the personal difficulties he faced during his reign and the struggle of fighting the Thirty Years' War (1618–48), and died here. Built in the Dutch Renaissance style its most impressive features are the tall towers, the well-preserved interior decoration and the huge royal collections of riding equipment, glass and porcelain.

EGESKOV CASTLE

Kvaerndrup, Denmark

Egeskov was built for the statesman Frands Brockenhuus on an artificial island of oak piles in the middle of a lake because of the chronic instability in the region. It was finished in 1554. Designed as two independently defendable houses, it was connected by a double wall containing hidden staircases, and could only be reached by a drawbridge. Restored in the late 1800s the Egeskov was converted into a state-of-the-art working farm, and now also houses a vintage car museum.

KRONBORG CASTLE

Elsinore, Denmark

Kronborg, where Shakespeare set Hamlet, stands on the furthest edge of Zealand overlooking the tiny 4-km (2.5-m) wide strait between Denmark and Sweden, the entrance to the Baltic. It dates back to a castle built in the 1420s to levy customs. Frederick II (1559–88) completely rebuilt Kronborg as a Renaissance palace, restored by Christian IV after a fire in 1629. Sweden captured Kronborg in 1658, which afterwards had to have massive new defences added. Later it served as a slave prison.

GRIPSHOLM CASTLE

Stockholm, Sweden

Only part of a wall survives from the original Gripsholm Castle, built by Bo Jonsson, one of Sweden's most important officials, next to Lake Mälaren (Sweden's third largest) in 1380. The powerful King Gustavus I (1523–60) rebuilt the castle as a proper fortress with towers and it remained in the Swedish royal family. Used as a prison for much of the eighteenth century it was completely renovated in the late nineteenth century. Today it houses Sweden's National Portrait Gallery.

Eastern Europe

The political upheaval in Eastern Europe of recent years is only one more episode in a remarkable history of instability stretching back over centuries.

Spissky Hrad, which preserves one of the most impressive medieval defensive complexes in the whole of Europe, dates back to the Middle Ages when Slovakia was ruled by the Hungarian Magyars before it too was absorbed into the Austro-Hungarian Empire. Poland has had an extremely well-defined sense of national identity for centuries but in the Middle Ages power in the area was really vested in the wealthy and influential cities of the Hanseatic League, which lasted from the twelfth century to 1669 and controlled the lucrative Baltic Sea trade. The enormous castle at Malbork gave the city its power in the League.

The most modern of all the castles in this section, Peles in Romania, belongs to the time when Romania was created as a new independent country in 1878 after centuries in which the region had been ruled by the Ottoman Turks and the Austrian Hapsburgs. It is only appropriate, then, that Carol I of Romania died at Peles on 10 October 1914, just a few weeks after the First World War began and brought the last traces of medieval Europe to an end.

MALBORK CASTLE
Gdasnk, Poland

The Teutonic 'Order of Knights of Mary in Jerusalem' established the sprawling castle of Malbork by the River Nogat in 1274, using bricks thanks to a lack of local stone. But it took 230 years to complete the complex of three castles and defences, which now covers an area four times bigger than Windsor Castle. The 3,000 knights who lived there used it to collect customs duties on river traffic. Badly damaged in the Second World War, Malbork has been fully restored.

KARLSTEJN CASTLE
Beroun, Czech Republic

Only 30 km (18 miles) southwest of Prague, Karlstejn was built by the King of the Romans Charles IV (1346–78) to house the state archives and crown jewels. Set on a high point in the valley of the Berounka, the castle was remodelled in the Gothic style in the sixteenth century and again in the nineteenth. Today its most imposing feature is the large rectangular main tower, and the Holy Cross chapel with 128 wooden-panel paintings and 2,200 precious stones set in plaster.

BRAN CASTLE
Brasov, Romania

Bran Castle in Transylvania is famously the legendary home of Count Dracula, based on the real Vlad III 'the Impaler' (1431–76). The castle existed by 1377, playing a vital role in defending the Hungarians from the Ottoman Empire and the Tartars. By the sixteenth century Bran was a fortified trading centre. The castle, now in Romania, is a curious mix of stone and timber, creating an interior with overhanging galleries, windows and teetering tiled roofs, while the castle's towers overlook the surrounding countryside.

PELES CASTLE
Sinaia, Romania

Pure fantasy, Peles Castle combines Gothic, Renaissance, Baroque, and Rococo styles and is built of wood, stone, marble and brick. It was begun in 1873 on the orders of Prince Carol I of Romania and was finished after the war that made Romania independent and him king. Surrounded by seven terraces and other buildings including stables, a hunting lodge, and its own electricity generating plant, Peles also contains themed chambers like the Turkish Room, and collections of porcelain, paintings, chandeliers and stained glass.

SPISSKY HRAD
Spissky Hrad, Slovakia

Clinging to the top of a 634-m (2,080-ft) high hill Spissky Hrad ('Spiss Castle') is a huge fortified stronghold, still standing in isolated magnificence, its white walls contrasting with the green slopes. Spissky Hrad was certainly in existence by 1120 when it defended Hungary's northern border. Over succeeding centuries more and more was added until the castle had one of the largest ranges of medieval military architecture in Europe. It was destroyed by fire in 1780 and restoration started in 1970.

Index